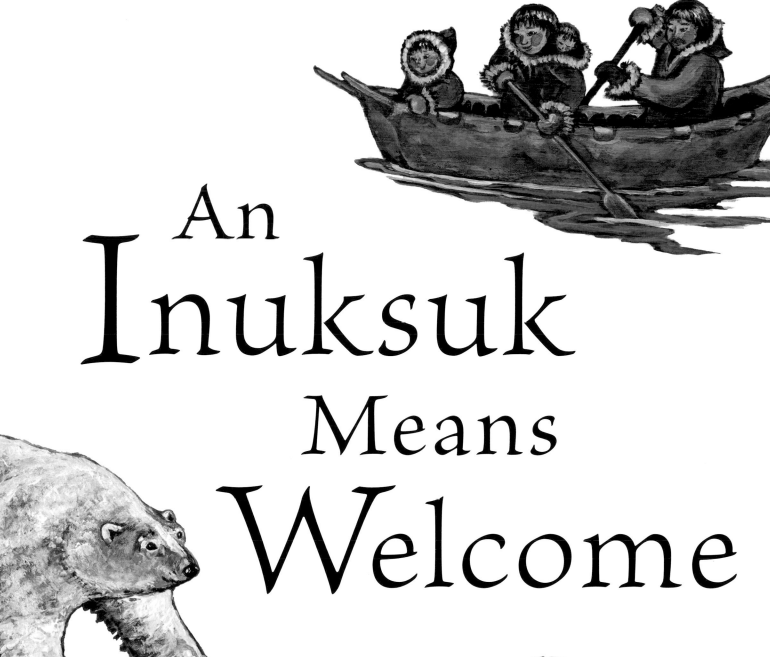

An Inuksuk Means Welcome

WORDS & ART BY

Mary Wallace

Owlkids Books

Thanks to Timmun and Kristiina Alariaq and their family for sharing their passion for our North and its traditional Inuit knowledge.

Acknowledgments

To my parents, who immigrated to Canada. They taught me that a home can be made in any place, time, or space, as long as there is a circle of people who love and care for one another.

For children everywhere, and for the adults who share caring words with them, in all the languages of our global village.

Selected Bibliography

Allan Angmarlik (Inuit Heritage Trust), in conversation with the author.

Hallendy, Norman. "Inuksuit: Semalithic Figures Constructed by Inuit in the Canadian Arctic." *Threads of Arctic Prehistory: Papers in Honour of William E. Taylor Jr.* David Morrison and Jean-Luc Pilon, eds. Canadian Museum of Civilization: Gatineau, Quebec, 1994.

———. *Inuksuit: Silent Messengers of the Arctic.* Vancouver: Douglas & McIntyre, 2001.

Peter Taqtu Irniq (former Commissioner of Nunavut), in conversation with the author.

Timmun and Kristiina Alariaq (owners and operators of Huit Huit Tours), in conversation with the author.

Owlkids Books acknowledges the financial support of the Canada Council for the Arts, the Ontario Arts Council, the Government of Canada through the Canada Book Fund (CBF) and the Government of Ontario through the Ontario Media Development Corporation's Book Initiative for our publishing activities.

Published in Canada by
Owlkids Books Inc.
10 Lower Spadina Avenue
Toronto, ON M5V 2Z2

Published in the United States by
Owlkids Books Inc.
1700 Fourth Street
Berkeley, CA 94710

Library and Archives Canada Cataloguing in Publication

Wallace, Mary, 1950-, author
       An Inuksuk means welcome / Mary Wallace.

Text in Inuktitut language and English.
ISBN 978-1-77147-137-4 (bound)

       1. Inuktitut language--Alphabet--Juvenile literature. 2. Inuktitut language--Juvenile literature.
I. Title.

PM55.W35 2015   j497'.124   C2014-908271-1

Library of Congress Control Number: 2014958764

Edited by: Jessica Burgess
Designed by: Alisa Baldwin
Inuktitut consultant: Noel McDermott

Manufactured in Shenzhen, China, in May 2015, by C&C Joint Printing Co.
Job #201500158R1

A   B   C   D   E   F

Publisher of Chirp, chickaDEE and OWL
www.owlkidsbooks.com

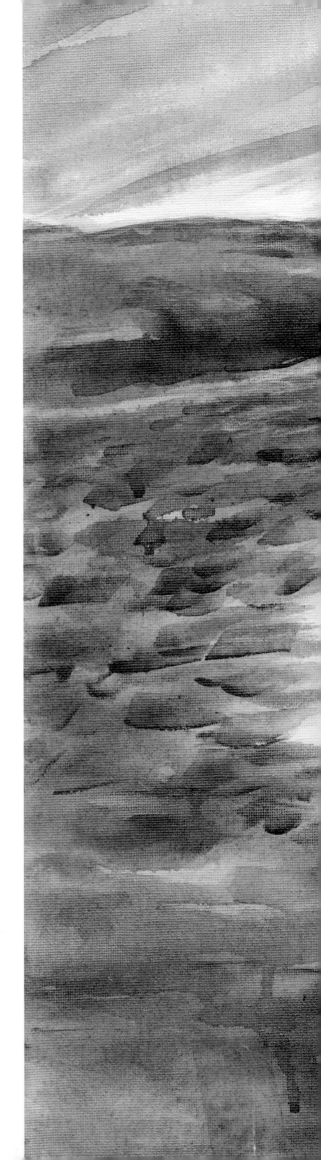

For thousands of years, people living in the Arctic have built stone towers called inuksuit to guide them across this land of snow and ice. A single marker is called an inuksuk. It can mark where to find food or how to get home. It can even be a way of saying, "Welcome."

In this book, each letter of the word **inuksuk** is represented by an Inuktitut word. Together, the letters create an overview of life in the Arctic. Look for inuksuit to guide you as you read.

I

is for inuksuk,

the stone messenger
that stands at the top
of the world.

I

ee-nuck-shuck

ᐃᓄᒃᓱᒃ

N

is for nanuq,

the powerful polar
bear of the North.

na-nuck

ᑕᕝᑫᑊᒃ

U

is for umiaq,

the family's summer
sea boat.

U

oo-me-ak

ᐅᒥᐊᖅ

K

is for kamik,

a warm waterproof
boot made from seal
and caribou skin.

K

ka-meek

ᑭᒻᒥᒃ

S

is for siku,

the Arctic sea ice
that changes with
the seasons.

S

see-koo

ᒥᑯ

U

is for umimmat,

the shaggy muskoxen
that share the tundra
with other wildlife.

U

oo-mim-mat

ᐅᒥᖕᒪᑦ

K

is for kunik,

a soft kiss that says
we're family.

K

koo-nik

ᑯᓂ�7

An inuksuk means welcome...
...but inuksuit can mean many other things, too.

ᐃᓄᖕᒍᐊᖅ
Inunnguaq (in-nung-wok) means "image statue." It is built in the shape of a person. It lets people know that someone has been there before them or that they are on the right path.

ᓂᑭᓱᐃᑦᑐᖅ
Nikisuittuq (ni-ki-sweet-tuck) means "North Star." It points to the North Star in the winter sky.

ᓇᒃᑳᑕᐃᑦ
Nakkatait (nak-ka-ta-eet) means "things that fell in water." It points to a good place to fish.

ᖃᔭᒃᑯᕕᒃ
Qajakkuvik (ka-ya-ko-vik) means "kayak rests." It is a place to store a kayak while it dries.

ᐱᕈᔭᖃᕐᕕᒃ
Pirujaqarvik (pi-roo-ya-kar-vik) means "where the meat cache is." This stone marker shows where meat is stored.

ᑐᑉᔭᒃᖓᐅᑦ
Tupjakangaut (toop-ya-kang-out) means "footsteps of game." It steers hunters toward good places to find animals to hunt.

ᐃᓄᒃᓱᒃ ᖁᕕᐊᓱᒃᑐᖅ
Inuksuk quviasuktuq (ee-nuck-shuck ko-vee-a-suck-tuck) means "inuksuk expressing joy." It is built to express the joy of the place and the builder.

Did you see some of these inuksuit in the pages of this book?